The Journey Tree

A Journey into Old Age

MARY PETERSON

WESTBOW
PRESS®
A DIVISION OF THOMAS NELSON
& ZONDERVAN

WestBow Press books may be ordered through booksellers or by contacting:

WestBow Press
A Division of Thomas Nelson & Zondervan
1663 Liberty Drive
Bloomington, IN 47403
www.westbowpress.com
844-714-3454

ISBN: 978-1-6642-0807-0 (sc)
ISBN: 978-1-6642-0808-7 (e)

Print information available on the last page.

WestBow Press rev. date: 11/23/2020

Contents

Dedication

To Walter Peterson, my husband of 50 years and to Christine Wright, my best friend of more than 20 years. Both of whom I expected to grow old with me.

To my husband, who always thought I could do anything I put my mind to. And was there with support. He filled my life with love and joy. To others, he filled theirs with riddles. He told them anytime and anywhere; parties, church, airplane, Amtrak or wherever an opportunity came up.

To my friend with whom I shared so many good times and secrets that will never be told. Memories of the times we spent around her dining room table talking about everything under the sun, including our children while cracking and eating nuts. I remember how we laughed when we were described as the "black power" during our time working together.

Acknowledgements

Many thanks to my family and friends for their support. They were there when I wrote my first book. And encouraged me when I talked about wanting to write another. Sometimes thank you are words too inadequate. I say mine sincerely with love and appreciation.

Thanks to my granddaughter Cayla in California who was my sounding board. Her feedback was so helpful in putting some parts together. Or hearing her say "That's good, Nana." kept me motivated.

To my son Pete for steering me in the right direction when I had problems on the computer regardless of the time. And was always ready with advice. Also for taking several photo shots before we were satisfied.

And to my daughter Cathy who inspires me without even knowing it. She has a big heart, willing to share and always ready to give advice to others.

Last but not least, to my friends and my new acquaintances who so willingly allowed me to interview them. And all who gave me feedback about their journey. Reading each gave me a different idea of what was needed. There was joy, sadness, humor and overall reality. I would not have wanted to do this book without that combination.

Introduction

I am still on my journey. How about you? Allow me to talk to you throughout this book. Each of our journeys are different and all will not start at the same time. Together we will walk or run though the good times, the not so good times, the bad times and all those unforgettable times in between. Also, we will be able to recognize all that is still going on in our lives. Look at it like it is a new job and sitting down time is limited. Where would be the best place or time in our lives to start telling about our journeys? First I thought age 40 or maybe 50 would be a good age to say our journey started. But why not earlier? For some, due to circumstances or happenings in their lives, they began to feel old at 20 or 25 and wonder where it was leading them. I found out that some agree. To me that sounded so young, but what age doesn't when you are pushing eighty. I can truthfully say at those ages, I was definitely not thinking about getting old. Instead I had my mind on getting a boyfriend. Wait a minute, I should say a serious one and falling in love. Maybe I should add getting a decent job, maybe a husband and later finding a baby sitter so I could go out. I could name a few more, but none relating to getting old. Let me see if I can break it down. At age 40 we celebrate the big 4-0 and even celebrate with a big "throw down" party. Why this birthday is made such a fuss over, I don't know. I'll have to ask some of the ladies who talk to me about their journey.

I asked a few friends, a new acquaintance and a few relatives to tell about their journey to old age in my book. Maybe the words "old age" frightens some. But I believe once we get past the age thing, all anyone should be able to see is the blessings. The ones sharing their journey will be funny, heartbreaking and serious at times. You will see some of my poetry writing that fits the stories as told. We all will eventually have to face those changes that comes with aging; bad eyes, aches and pains, a different way of walking and maybe an added pound or two. No longer will you have that little swish and certain sway of your hips that you use to have and men, you'll notice a little change in your walk, too. And I believe there are other things going on that you only you know. But, I have to say, we will continue to look good at the age of 65 or plus. And hold on, we can still catch the eye of a man or a woman. As you read through this book, I am hoping you will laugh and maybe feel connected with some of what the men and/or women felt while on their journey. In between our stories and recollections of our journeys, I will give information and surprises that are helpful to know about old age. Yes, I use that phase again, but it's alright. Before you finish, you will have a lot more to add about who you are now and all you are able to do regardless of your age. You will have to agree, you are some kind of wonderful. Then when you hear someone make the comment, "Age "ain't" nothing but a number," you'll high five them and say "You got that right."

Be still and see the beauty of God's work

These are the thoughts that were going through my mind when I chose the title, "The Journey Tree." I only had to glance to see how beautiful and strong God has made a tree. The time comes when a tree changes, just like us. The different shapes of leaves change to all different kinds of colors. They don't seem to be in any particular hurry. For a short while, the trees are full of beautiful leaves and slowly they fall off, only to return in the spring. The tree and the leaves represent our senior days. It tells how colorful our lives are now and as you look back over the past how different. Today I picked up a leaf and looked at it expecting to see one of the usual Fall colors; orange, red, yellow or the brown. This leaf had all of the colors with different shades of each. And it was beautiful. The poet, Joyce Kilmer wrote this and I think it fits us well. A Tree-- "I think that I should never see a poem lovely as a tree. A tree whose hungry mouth is prest against the earth's sweet flowing breast." We are like that tree, lovely and inhaling all the love and knowledge that we can pass on. We don't fall into aging in a few weeks. God gives us time to grow old gracefully, be always grateful and enjoy this blessing.

Several women and men were asked to tell me about their journey into old age for my book. Some looked offended and others would say "I'm not old." I would laugh with them and say, "Yes you are." Of course I put it a little differently. Maybe I said "as you got older."

However, I did get some feedback to include. I believe you will enjoy reading what they have to say.

This is good place to talk about the notable and not so notable changes in our bodies and lives that happened as we got older. We are no longer the social butterfly we once were, nor do we have the energy or the desire to be one. And that's alright. What we do have is the good sense to know we must keep moving, stay involved and enjoy every day. There are many changes in our lives, some good and some bad. You will read about them as you go through this book.

I have come to the conclusion that it is up to the individual to say when their journey started. Many of us have unspeakable dramatic events that happened early in our lives. You look back and realize this was part of your journey. Almost everything that happened was a part of it. Therefore making a way for you to reach an older and wiser age. These happenings, no doubt made you stronger and more insightful. For some, religion helped make the journey easier. For others it may have been a partner, spouse or children. Maybe there is some part in your journey where you can look back and add laughter to something that happened on your path. Once you have read my friend and relative's account of her journey, you'll have to agree.

"Finding Strength Is Not Always Easy"

My title for her story is **"Finding Strength Is Not Always Easy"**

And she told it like this. My old age started at 50, when I saw so many gray hairs coming in faster than I could count them. After that, it was my dentures and using Fixodent so they would not slip around (ha ha) when I was talking and singing. And while going through this age journey, I had to keep a prayer on my lips and in my heart. I mean real hard as my best friends; my Mom's death and then my sweetheart, loving husband's death. The lost of my closest loves back to back. Oh, how I prayed. But God said, "No, they are mine and I am calling them. And I will be there for you as I have been all the time. This made my journey harder because I didn't think I could go on by myself. But, along the journey, I found out others care about me more than I realized. Oh, talking about Arthritis. I realized I had loads of it when I got up and couldn't move until I straighten out first so I could move. Than I had to get replaced joints. Oh Lord, that's when I really knew arthritis had made reservation in my body. I knew I was getting old or already old when I didn't realize my partial denture in front was missing. There is a story behind this. I

3

went to church that morning and out to lunch with a few friends afterwards. They kept looking at me and I wondered why until I was wiping my mouth and felt my partial missing. I asked why they didn't tell me. Their answer, "You came to church like that. We thought you knew." I looked everywhere and couldn't find it. They said, "Girl you must have ate it." I tried getting out of going to church that next Sunday but it was said, "You went last Sunday with your teeth missing." God has always played a role in my life, all through my life time. Especially when I asked Him into my life and having a personal relationship with Him. So, as I journey through life I could talk with Him during every stage of my life; teens, middle and old/older.

C. James of New Jersey

It's my imagination!

When I was flying home from California, 38,000ft in the air, my thoughts drifted as I watched the clouds. As fluffy and white as they were, a little light brown would creep in, but the fluffy clouds would continue to move along with them. It was something about the clouds moving slowly as though they were saying relax. Even with a little brown, it didn't keep the sun from shining through at times. Nor did it stop the clouds from drifting to whatever direction they were headed. And drifting is alright, as long as it doesn't slow us down too much. That's what we want to tell our bodies as we slowly walk toward reaching fifty plus. Many of us could still have teenage children to raise at age forty. I graduated from nursing school when I was slightly over forty years old. For a while I was the talk of the barber shop. Yes, not the beauty shop. Men talk, too. The reason why I tell this is because it was said, I was "too old" to go back to school. Even then, some viewed forty as old.

Age forty, (not 49 or 50)☺ is when I think my journey to old age really begun. By then I had been married twenty whole years with two grown children. Honestly, I still didn't think much about getting old. Of course it crossed my mind ever so often, but it didn't slow me down, well not much anyway. In some places in our society it classifies us at age fifty-five as a senior and AARP allows you to join at fifty. And that's good for all the needed information seniors could use. At that time I was feeling no way like a senior. I was working every day and even managed to get out on the dance floor with my husband. But I have to say I was *getting old*.

That's another topic or should I say *a play of words*. When did we stop saying, "I'm getting old" to "I'm old?" Of course if you're seventy y/o and can pass for fifty or sixty, you might want to skip this. On the other hand, take it anyway. Outside appearance is great, but your body may still say seventy. If you're not sure, play this choice game to see which side get the most checks. I did and was surprised at ~~my~~ choices.

I say *"I'm getting old"* when	I say *"I'm old"* when
I try to do something but can't	I quit trying because I know better
I can't' walk as fast as I use to	I walk a short distance and rest
It's hard for me to sit low	It takes me longer to get up
I can't stay up late at night	I need a little extra sleep or rest
My joints start aching	I have to have replacements
Partying is no longer appealing	I admit I can no longer "hang"
My prescription bottles increase	my perfume bottles decrease
I cover my gray hair with color	I wear gray hair like I earned it
I'm looking for a woman/man my age	I look for a younger woman/man
I mention my aches & pains	My talk is all about aches & pains
My hair start falling out	There's more bald spots then hair
I wear glasses to see better	I need glasses with bifocals
I try to hold my stomach in	Holding in no longer work

Start of a Journey/ who's to say when

Of course we knew our journey was not always going to be easy. There were times we didn't want to accept what was happening. Along the way there were hardships, times when you wanted to make a joyful noise and many times when others came into your life to make it turn out either way. All I'm saying is, "Your journey is your journey." The next writer carries us from the very beginning and touches on the different phases of her journey to her present active senior years. She titled hers, **"My Journey."**

And she has this to say. We move through life as through a journey. Our paths unfold differently. Some are filled with joy and clarity, while the journey of others are filled with anguish, difficulty and uncertain experiences. My journey has been a mixture of all of these. It started in Montgomery, Alabama where I was born. I was raised by two wonderful family members who had also raised my mother. I was loved, nurtured, disciplined and given a wonderful foundation by them. They were my angels. My spiritual journey started very early. I was taken to Sunday school, church services, Baptist training union, Sunbeams and anything that occurred at church. I have continued my church life participating in all activities that would enhance my Christian growth and is married to a minister.

My education leg of the journey began in Matthews, Alabama. It was a small school in a rural area where my mother, Mary Frances Huffman was the principal. We boarded at a family home in the area during school days and on weekend went home via greyhound bus. Education was a top priority in my home. I graduated from Alabama State College Laboratory High School at age 15 and then to Stillman College. I met some obstacles there because of my age and never being away from home. So I sucked it up and moved on. I received my degree in Elementary Education at age 18 and later two master degrees and have worked on my doctorate.

My family was very active in the civil rights movement. One that stood out in my mind was the Montgomery bus boycott with Mrs. Rosa Parks and Dr. Martin Luther King. Each Monday night we would attend the informative Mass meetings. I was there with lots of other children. I did not understand the full scope of things, but I did know that as Black people we were being mistreated. I continued this part of my journey when I grew up; participating in marches, sit-ins, voter registration, etc. This part of my journey was probably the most dangerous. But I look back and say, I am glad I was a Foot Solider for the cause of freedom. The career part of my journey took me into the classroom for 42 years. There I found myself not just being a teacher, but a mother, nurse, confident, you name it. I felt so proud when they successfully managed the concepts they were being taught.

Lastly my spiritual journey or my walk with God. This part of my journey is the most important. I gave my life to Christ at age six. And since then He has guided and directed my path. This part of my journey has taught me that I need God's hand to lead me, strengthen me and give me courage. When my plans are disrupted, he lets' me know that maybe it was my plan and not his. It is amazing and incredible how God loves us, how sufficient his grace is and how he understands all. I would take nothing for this part of my journey.

Who am I?
God's Servant
Patricia Day Smoke

Changes—"There's No Stopping Us Now"

The best place to start is with our *Social life style changes*

But, hear me now, this is not a bad thing. As we begin getting just a little bit older, our bodies began to have less energy for the strenuous activities we once did. Some of these may sound familiar. Those three or four miles around the track is now down to maybe two. And you are getting out of breath when you climb more than a few stairs. Remember when you played golf and walked around the course? Now using the golf cart is so much better. Maybe at forty you were still able to play a little basketball and every now and then make a basket. All that running and jumping is not as much fun as it used to be. But in your day, you could keep up with the best of them. While on the subject of activities that take your breath away, let's not forget about dancing. Some of you might remember that song lyric, "Let me see you move it on the dance floor, baby." And you can still move it, but how and how much depends on you. So your social life is winding down and perhaps that's a good thing for many of us. There is more time to spend with your very active grandchildren, learn something new that is less strenuous, go on bus trips and not worry about the driving. Now you can be a backseat driver ☺while your husband or someone else is driving. One more idea that is fun for all ages and it won't tire you out. The X Box is a visual game that includes bowling, basketball, tennis, exercise and even boxing. And sometimes, you could end up winning over those younger folks.

Here is something else to think about socializing. Do some of you remember when almost everything was done by hand and at a much slower pace? Now all of that has changed, and we should have more time to just sit and visit. Some of us do that. But, the thing is, now that we are old (have to use that word again) ☺ or getting old, we find ourselves wanting to be involved in many different things. With all your life experiences, some organizations, community clubs and church clubs would welcome you in. For some, being involved in your grandchildren's life and those who are close to you is the joy of it all. To sum it all up, your social life is not dependent on your age. It is what you want to do and can do. After all, you are individuals separate in your strength and your ability to do what's right for you. So many ladies our age continues to be active, attractive and smart in so many ways. I enjoy the TV celebration, "Black Girls Rock" but I want to see one titled "Black Seniors Rock **And** Roll." I'm not talking about all celebrities. Instead mix it up with every day seniors, men and women in our communities who has accomplished a great deal and continues to hold it together.

Beauty and Aging

This is a good place to talk about *Beauty and Aging.*

Of course these two go together. No question about it. It doesn't matter if you are a little bent over or your hair is thinning or your nails are not long and pretty like they once were. A nail salon can fix that. Maybe you don't have that bounce in your step or that walk that says "I'm cool." What you do have is what's on the inside and outside. I'm not talking about having the latest haircut and clothes that look super good on you, but the confident look that says "I've been there and done that and look at me now." This heading fits so many men and women in their senior years. You have beauty on the inside because of all the things you do for your family and others and because of that, it shows on the outside. When you spot a senior at an affair or a funeral, look at the men. They look handsome in their suits and matching ties and not a shirt tail hanging out. The ladies could easily pass for five or maybe eight years younger. Of course you can try one or two of those products advertised on TV. How many of those commercials have you seen about creams that will give you younger looking skin? How about the one that will rid you of wrinkles around your eyes and under your neck. There is one where you can grow longer lashes and I am sure there are plenty more beauty aid or fixer uppers out there. My question is, have you tried any of these or been tempted? I am not against any of these remedies. They may work for some and not for others. At an early age you wore makeup perhaps just to look more grown up and your parents would say you didn't need it. Maybe, you used it to enhance your beauty or cover blemishes or put a little color on your cheeks. There is nothing wrong with that. As you got older, you needed a little more help and gradually the need for all of that lessened. Some of you see yourself with just lipstick and some color on your cheeks with a little eye liner to make up for those thinning lashes. It might be a release to some to use soap and water and call it a day. What it all comes down to is this. The aging part is there and it's not going away, but the beauty of it is that we can still hold it all together. If we want to socialize, stay involved and look presentable, we have to give it some thought.

A Dress Code for seniors!

But, no one told me there was *A Dress Code for seniors!*

"Do you think this dress is too young looking? Am I too old for it?" You're hesitant about buying the dress, but you really like it. Have you ever been shopping and overhead this? Perhaps heard it from someone you were with or said or thought about it yourself. Maybe, just maybe, you have a friend that will tell you, "You're too old for that dress." I know for a fact clothes are not labeled with an age on them or have special racks/sections marked for specific ages. Only thing I notice is size and care instructions. Besides, you'll know if half of your back is out or the cleavage is so low you're afraid to bend over. Or it was something you wouldn't wear even if you were thirty years younger. If you are still hesitant, you look at the material. It wants to hug you in all the wrong places. Yes, it's your size and you start to wonder what's happening here. Parts of your body seems to be more abundant in places and less in others. Have you noticed that parts of your body take on a different shape as you get older? It's hard sometimes to notice the physical changes on your body. Who wants to take the time to do a body check daily or as often as we should? Some of your steps are shorter when you walk instead of those long strides. Of course that was in younger days, but you knew you still had it going on. What about the material they use now? It wants to hug your body in places you don't. We know how to make it work; camouflage, camouflage, camouflage! Now you ask about the length.

Too short is maybe not what you want if the dress shows your knees. Unless you still have those legs that are long and gorgeous. Then go for it. But after all is said and tried on, the answer must come from you.

Since shoes are an important part of any outfit, let's talk about them. Do you remember wearing high heels, the higher the better and the stiletto heels? The high heels were 3 inches or more and now most of us are wearing the 1.5 inch heel or flats. When you are around seventy, give or take a few years, you might still be able to manage walking with an attitude ☺ in shoes that high. But are you walking in comfort or do the shoes look great but not feeling so good? You can't wait to take them off. Some of you can't remember the last time you wore them. Although there is some of us that can still manage. It was a gradual lowing of the heel for most of us. The pump came in style and then the lower heel and that was it for most of us. We knew we must do it for comfort and safety, while not taking away from the outfit. Did you think for a minute that you might be shrinking a little? It happens, but not to all of us. We can agree that stilettos are out. But ladies, we still have a chose. Buy higher heels and take a chance of falling or tripping or buy a lower heel and get more comfort and less chance of falling. Say to yourself, "My heels are lower but I still look good." Perhaps as women and seniors we find ourselves asking is the heels too flat or too high and do they match my hand bag and my outfit?

Do you ever wonder if men go thru all of this or is it just shirt and tie, pants and a nice pair of shoes? When they reach senior age, what are they thinking when they shop or have to dress for an affair? Do their wives or girlfriend help pick out what they wear or buy? Plenty of questions and I know some of you have the answer. From my close observation, the ones that I see at different functions have no problems at all looking well put together with or without help.

From a head full of hair to none at all

Is it true the first thing others look at when they see you is your hair/head and feet? At least, that's what I was always told. ☺ As for hair, there is so many remedies for bad hair days. As for me, a hat is number one. You can go natural, a real short hair cut or a boy cut, braids and extensions. Wigs are in. Gone are the days when they were made out of anything and you could tell at a glance it was a wig. Today, wigs are made out of human hair and other materials and in any color, style or length. None of these have an age limit. But have you noticed how some look so natural and on others, it just look like a wig. That would be me. ☺ Here's another thing to think about. Everyone doesn't want to go gray. But it so happens that they have no choice. You know how that is, you wake up one morning and there is a few strains of gray and it kept coming. Before you know it, you have more gray than you want. Besides, some thought it made them look old. There were ways to cover the gray with hair color. But, once colored, you have to keep it up, otherwise that gray will reappear. A friend of mine decided not to use color on her hair anymore and gradually her hair was all gray and beautiful. After receiving many comments about how pretty her gray hair was, more began to wear their white hair as it grew in. I say it's up to the individual and how they feel and want to look.

Now with the men, it's a whole other story. When men began to grow gray hair, it most often is around the edges. On them it look like someone or as I liked to think, God has sprinkled white dust through their hair. No matter where, they look distinguished. But on the other side of the coin, some have been known to use a little color. It's whatever look you want; the bald head, some may wear theirs a little long and others to the barber shop for a cut of their choice. Ladies have you noticed that under or on your chin a stray hair or two popping up when you least expect. Pull out those tweezers. How is it that some men look good with a face full of hair and we start plucking at the first sight? But, that's just how it is. Women shave unwanted hair from all parts of their body, starting from the legs to eyebrows. Why do some get gray hair earlier than others? There are a few theories besides age. Some suggest, it could be your nerves, hereditary or just meant to be. Some of this may be true. So I googled it to find out why some get gray earlier than others. According to research men may get gray hair as early as thirty years old whereas women at age thirty-five. Have you heard someone say that he or she is the cause of this gray hair on my head? Some of that may be true along with smoking and a vitamin deficiency. Some researchers found it could be caused by chronic stress, not just plain ole stress that's here today and gone tomorrow. But the kind of stress that last a long time and is recurring. I could give you all the scientific facts about how as we get older, pigment cells on hair follicles slowly begin to die. But just know, other than the three main reasons and there may be more, you have no control. So what do you do? I say, work with it.

And that's exactly what you have to do as you go through life's challenges.

When asked to tell about her journey, this next friend told it like it was just yesterday. As I read it, I immediately thought of all the challenges she must have faced. She did not put an age at the start of her journey and perhaps was not even ready for it to start. But it did and it brought to my mind that saying, "If you get lemons, make lemonade." There is no time frame for things to happen in your life, they just do. Which tells us, we are not in control. But, God helps us with His guidance.

"The Persistence of a Christian"

This is the title I used for her story: **"The Persistence of a Christian"**

*My life journey started when I was a youth and became a mother to eight of my siblings because our father died and our mother had to become the father role. Since then my journey has been about caring for others. I developed a prayer life early, because I went from being a daughter, sister, mother, grandmother and great grandmother. Only God knows how often I have prayed to Him for help and guidance. Thank God I was able to leave home and get an education that prepared me to deal with my life then and now. I've had my shares of life's ups and downs (deaths, sickness, heartaches, disappointments) but God brought me through. By being a single woman all my life, I have had love, joy and happiness along the way. If I were to tell the whole story of my life, you would be reading for days. Now that I am getting older, moving slower, eyesight dimmer and thinking, well I'm just not going there at this time. I will say, "It is not like it was yesterday." As for my social life, church responsibilities and being a Black Entrepreneur and traveling, I'm still doing it all. Yes, I am getting a little slower at things at the age of seventy-two, but I am still able to enjoy doing all those things. And I can thank God that I can still say, "I am going to continue living so God can use me for whatever, anywhere and anytime!"

Rosetta Ferguson/Morganton

"Digging Deep"

Sometimes when thinking about the old days, where we are now and how it use to be, we want to share. Sometimes we have to laugh a little, so I came up with these spoken words.

"Digging Deep"

When you started on this journey, you
knew you couldn't turn around
There would be places you've never been
before on unfamiliar ground
Then decided to dig a little deeper and this is what you found
You heard of the many changes that was sure to come your way
Did not think you were up to that, but now you can have your say

I'll be ok with the gray hair, "Nice & Easy" will take care of that
The arthritis pain is something else and will need more than a pat
I just had to dig a little deeper to find these remedies
With a cream here and a spray there, I
can move without much pain
Bring it on "old age" I saw you coming,
try stopping me with the rain

It's not all about the signs of aging, when
my steps start slowing down

It won't stop my happy times, I'll keep
going without much of a frown
Why not dig a little deeper to decide this is what I'll do
I will handle disappointments and whatever else comes my way
While traveling through life, I must move to welcome each day

After all this is my journey, yet I seem to have no control
That is why living life to the fullest is my ultimate goal
I could dig a little deeper but the fact will remain the same
Where it will take me next, the plan clearly is not mine
My journey is not over yet and with me that's just fine

When I look back at all the changes that occurred on my path, I was well on my journey when I reached my early sixties. Planning was now a part of getting things done. One of the most important part of my plans were to become more involved in the church. My friend Christine W. and I worked at Broughton Hospital for 30 years, working every other weekend. Therefore church was out most of the time. We promised ourselves when we retired that we would go to church every Sunday and become more involved. Both of us made good on that promised. Even then, I thought nothing about being old. On my journey, I look at it as going through three stages. First one, *resistance*. When someone would offer to help, lift something heavy, reach high or carry for me, I would quickly say, "That's alright, I can do it." Now the reaching I had to give into first. I shrunk just a little, (that's another sign of aging for some of us) and could no longer reach the high stuff. Now when I am shopping, I don't hesitate to ask someone to get something that's too high for me to reach. The second is *denial*. My famous line when someone would remark on my age would be, "I'm not old." OK, I know I questioned others for saying that. ☺ Besides I could back it up with all that I could still do. The third is *acceptance* or one could call it, facing the facts. I am so happy and blessed that everything about being old is part of a special journey. It's not important what I can't do any more or that I can't do it as fast or as well. I am still able to do it. Take another look at the three stages and ask yourself if maybe one of them fits you and perhaps add a few of your own.

It's always helpful to have a sounding board

I was talking over my ideas for a new book with my Granddaughter, Cayla, who only a few days before graduated from UCSB. She asked, "Why can't their journey start earlier, maybe twenty-five or thirty years old instead of forty or fifty? I thought about it and it made sense. It made even more sense when I began to get responses from friends. Another of Cayla's ideas came from her remembering the times I talked to her about back doors and other treatment prior to integration. I understood where she wanted me to go with this during the time of integration. I recalled this one incident during my employment and it definitely was a part of my journey.

During my time working at Broughton Hospital as a registered nurse (I was forty three or four, not realizing my journey had already started.) I have to say this incident made a big impact on my journey. As supervisors we were assigned to cover the whole hospital on our shift; it was second shift for me. And if you are familiar with this hospital, you know it covered plenty of ground. When a problem came up on any of the numerous wards, you had to go there and handle it. The hospital campus is spread out. I was called to a ward to handle a situation with a visiting family member regarding the treatment for one of the patients. When I got there, the visitor looked at me and stated, "I asked to see the supervisor". I can't remember exactly how I responded. But I did let her know I was it. And the problem was handled with questions answered. This made an impact because of the timing and I ask myself why a person would think, I couldn't be the one in charge. Or who knows, that may not have been her reason. She might have had a different person to handle her complaints before. I know integration played a big part in my journey as it most likely did in yours, no matter who you are. Some things that happened years ago, you can remember because of the timing and this was one of them for me.

"Work in Progress"

Think about growing and getting older as *"Work in Progress"*

Although unbeknown when we are babies that our journey has already started. We wonder how that is possible with skin so soft, wrinkle free and our innocence. As we begin to age, giving no thought what so ever about getting old, changes are already taking place in our mind and body. Some of us are able to look back and know at what age or stage in our life the journey started. Why does that description "old age" seem to frighten some? Whatever changes you can cover up, it still comes up the same. Progress is the key word here. We went from having others solve our problems to coming up with a solution for ourselves. Work was no problem, we had been doing that since we were old enough to have a social security card. But the kind of work that is needed now at our age includes concentration, giving knowledgeable advice to those that ask or may not ask and teaching from all the experiences we now have. Now that you have read this far, you realize this book is not all about what we can no longer do at our age, but rather to give us praise for all that we have done and all that we are doing now. You will find out from friends that had a say in my book that they are still doing. Did I think some were surprised by my asking? Yes. And following their response, we laughed together about our age. Yes, because I have said often enough that I'm not old. Maybe I was the only one that was in denial. For me, denial fits. And that was when I had reached well past 65 and went through those stages I mentioned earlier; resistance, denial and finely acceptance. Are you with me?

Memories that last with a touch of humor

When I stay still long enough just to watch the clouds and sunshine, they never stop moving. It is as though they are trying to tell me something. My journey has been full of sunshine one minute and next there was so much happening in my life, a cloud or some clouds would move in. During my journey there were weddings, births and deaths in my family. My husband had been a part of my life for fifty years and when he died, it made me realize how quickly time goes by. I knew I was getting older when I stopped handling situations and stress the same way I did when I was a few years younger. I had been married 30 years when I seriously started my journey. Although in those years before, I went through a lot and know it made me stronger. You know how it is when you are young and so many things happen with your children, husband, relatives and close friends. But for me that would be a whole other book. I would even have to stop and say out loud "Did I survive all that drama?" The bigger question I need to answer is who and what effected my journey. The first thing comes to mind is that I was 50 and my husband thought he was still 40. ☺ But, that's alright. Allow me to regress a minute here. We sometimes went to this club called "Sundown" or some other place where there was dancing. When he asked me to dance and I said not now, he would move on. I might add, without hesitation and dance with someone else. That didn't bother me because I thought he was a wild dancer ☺and I most often couldn't keep up. How about you? Stop a minute and think about that something that either made you laugh or angry with your spouse. While you are thinking, I'll tell you another funny incident. When I was really angry and very young into this marriage, I would take some of his clothes and lay them at the end of our yard. Of course, he would bring them back in as soon as he saw them. ☺ Just saying that even at my old age, I still remember and can smile.

"I Believe"

Do you have words to describe someone that you know or have met along the journey in your life? It doesn't matter if it was years ago or a few weeks. As for me, when I think about strength, faith and having trust in God, my school friend of many years ago comes to mind. And when you read her letter you will understand why I say this. When I asked her would she write me about her journey to old age, she didn't hesitate. What can you say when others can look back at their past and all that happened on their journey and still say, **"I believe?"** She responded by writing me this letter.

Hello Mary,

When did I realize I was getting old? When I took my last child to school. The other mothers were young girls and I was the oldest mother there. Also when old man arthritis came upon my body and I couldn't do things like I used to do. Like reach up, my knees ached and it hurt to walk. Another thing was when my second daughter was in the 12th grade in school and was shocked that her mother was pregnant. She would go to the doctor with me. When our sweet baby girl was born, she was happy to have a sweet baby sister. They are all grown up now and they show their love for each other very well. I thank God for them and a wonderful husband and father to them all. Mary, please keep me in your prayers that if it is God's will, I will get better and get rid of this cancer. God bless you and thank you for your concern.

Love you much,
Connie
Chester, PA

What side are you taking?

I remember this one line of a poem I learned when I was real young. It read like this; "Remember that you have a mind in which you can decide, remember that your mind is free to follow either side."

Now as we continue to talk about our age and the journey we passed through, there are some things that make you say, "Maybe I am getting old, but I can still do a whole lot of things." It doesn't matter how many times you say "I'm not old", it doesn't change the fact that you are. You might not want to think so because you can still do certain things that you did when you were younger. Stop to think, maybe you can, but are you doing them at a slower pace and getting tired quicker? Regardless, the positive side is that it is good for you. Keep doing all those things that keep you going. I didn't say "keep you young." Stay active in whatever way you choose. The time and energy you spend with your grands and great grands, involvement in church and the community means so much. And, oh yes, you might have found a man/woman in your senior years. If so, good for you. Those for sure will keep you active both mentally and physically. So, like me, with some or all of the above, you still fall under the "old age category." Don't get upset, laugh with me. ☺ Your body knows it and the calendar acknowledges it. So does a clock. Although, we don't want to think of it just ticking away our younger days, instead time to plan what to do next. And guess what? It doesn't always have to be what's best for us, but what's the most fun.

"Hey Handsome/ Good Looking! What you got cooking?"

There's always something left for you to enjoy while letting someone do for you. I'm thinking about cooking. Something a lot of men didn't do while their wives were there to do it. Or it could be there were more out to eat occasions. Now, maybe things have changed and the situation is not the same. Men are doing a little more cooking. Instead of hearing the words, "What's for dinner, honey? We say, *"Hey Handsome/ Good Looking! What you got cooking?"*

There are several men that share the cooking with their spouse and enjoy doing it. Or just prepare a meal themselves. Ladies, as you are slowly reaching that comfortable age, how much cooking are you doing? Perhaps your answer will depend on some of these factors. You no longer have a spouse to fix for or now it's just the two of you. Your children have all left home, your grandchildren is over once in a while and you don't like eating alone much. These reasons are not meant to sound sad. There is an upside; you and your husband can go out to eat more often. That's a maybe. Just because you want to slow down on your cooking, he still wants that home cooked meal maybe a few days a week. What to do? What to do? Compromise. "It's just you and me now and there's no need to cook as much and as often. Let's go out once in a while." Here's another idea if you haven't already thought of it. Invite three or four friends over for a pot luck meal, nothing fancy. You remember how it was done when you were a little younger; eat, lively conversation and plenty of fun. If you are involved in your church, there is always an occasion to bring your favorite dish. There was a time when you had one. But now at this slowing down age you probably find it much easier to buy something already fixed. Of course, it's not as good. Without you doing all the fixing and cooking, it saves the wear and tear on the body. But, you have to admit, the homemade sweet potato pies, pound cakes, fried chicken and coleslaw can't be beat. Can you remember standing over that stove with a frying pan full of grease and frying chicken? Or going to the club "Sundown" on Saturday night getting that good ole greasy fried chicken sandwich. For those who are not familiar with this club, it was in the rural area and large enough for eating, drinking, dancing and having fun. And it no longer exist. Now, this is how it's done. You place your order a day or a few hours before it is needed, pick it up and your meal is ready for the table. Cooking is kind of a big deal and it seemed whomever retired first got that job.

Retirement!

Some might say that's part of the joy of aging. What do you think? Have you heard this question before? "You're retired, what are you doing now? Answer is nothing, I'm retired. That brings me to this next question. Have you ever wondered why many seniors continue to work after retiring? I found out some of the reasons and it made sense. Financial reasons (retirement check is not enough), boredom (enjoys being around other people and having something to do), really not ready to retire, but had the time in. Or it might not be any of those reasons. These are some reasons I found to be true. Also, those who you think are volunteers may be getting some pay for the job they are doing. Even if not, they seemed to enjoy doing it. The jobs are part time and not too strenuous. I know of a few, and I'm included, who found part time jobs after they retired. I soon found out I had to work harder on that job than I did on the job from which I retired. And for less money. ☺ I don't have to tell you how long that lasted. On a game show, one question was "What are the best things about getting old? One of the answers was retirement. Besides, retirement is all about being free to do some of the things you never had time to do before. You can choose from the reasons I heard and you probably know firsthand; sleep late, no time schedule, watch soap operas, play golf any time of the day, my own boss and dress how you want or maybe not at all if it's early in the morning. Now you have choices that you never dreamed of. You can stay up late to watch a movie and not worry about getting up early for work. Those are just a few of the things that you no longer have to be concerned about. It seems like only last year someone was asking "Who wants to go out to the old juke joints and drink beer?" Now, some might answer, "Not me, I need to get my rest. Those pickles and shots of bourbon give me the heartburn." ☺ Regardless of what one might think or do, retirement is part of the journey.

My heart, my love, the best of both

For some, their journey to an older age is like a testimony. Many can look back on all that has happened in their lives that brought them this far. The vivid memories of the different people that touched and is still touching their lives brings joy and sometimes sadness. It's easier now to realize the great impact our children made on our journey because we were so busy being sure they were fed and taken care of. Because your journey is not yet over, there will be more that touch your heart, your way of thinking and the good and not so good side of you. When asked about your journey to old age, one incident may stand out in your mind above all the others and you find yourself wanting to share.

After reading what this friend had to say, I could find no better heading then this: **"God is Always Watching"**

The following is how she chose to tell about her journey to an older age. She begins by saying,

> "He keeps on blessing me." At this age I know how true this is. I have things I do daily to keep me going, such as praying, reading, but most of all staying in prayer. My journey included the good times and the bad times. But I know whatever kind of day I'm having, I can hold onto His unchanging hand. Oh,

there have been days when I would do wrong things (and I knew they were wrong). Is it safe to say most of us or some of us at one time or another, have done this? I have always had a relationship with God, but for me it really started to grow when I started to work in the church. As time went by, I continued this. All of us have been through things we thought we could not get past. By the grace of God, we did. Being the strong Black women I am, there are still things that happened on my journey as I was getting older that made me stop and think. It took my youngest child to make me aware. When I was going through a health issue and still continuing to always do things for myself, I decided to go to the bathroom without asking for help. Well, my "strong self" fell in the floor. My youngest son had come home to help out until I got better. I was lying on the floor crying when he heard me. It just so happened my middle son came by and they got their Mama up and back to bed. There is an old saying "out of the mouth of babes" thus, my youngest son informed me of this. "Mama you always help everybody, let someone help you. It don't hurt to ask." He went on to say, "We are your kids and we will be here for you." And when my oldest child came in to help, I knew God was with me in every way. Always thank God every day for your blessings, I do.

G. from Morganton, NC

Take a good look at yourself

There is a huge difference in "Being out there" (as some refer to our younger days) and just Socialization. I know for a fact I am not out there anymore. You know what I mean, the parties, the dances, the little clubs and I mean it was only room to dance. Occasionally there were other places where you could stay on the floor and talk. You could get a sandwich and a cold beer or something a little stronger. That was so much fun. I don't know if age did it for you or if it was something else. It may have been those little "juke joints that closed down. For me, I have to say it was age. My husband and I didn't stop going to places where there was music and dancing, only we danced to a different beat and for me a little slower. We went to places that didn't have that good greasy fried chicken and a can of cold beer. I realized when those places stopped having any appeal to me was when I noticed I was moving slowly to old age. I was probably heading toward forty or slightly over. Now understand, I am only speaking for myself because I can remember my husband could dance the night away. But social life continues without the juke joints. Some friends and my husband and I would occasionally give a party. Gradually the house parties became fewer and fewer. All of us were getting older and now our parties were given for a reason such as a milestone birthdays like 50, 70 or 80 or an anniversary. By then our children wanted to give the party for us. And we found it wonderful because it was becoming harder to be the "hostess with the mostess." (old expression) It became even harder to give up my younger self as I was reaching the half way mark. After all 50 is not so old and if we are interesting enough, we might make the cover of AARP magazine. ☺.

"The Eyes Have it. Or do they?"

Just because you are 65 plus years, it doesn't mean you are in need of help with your eye sight. Although most of us do. Remember when we had 20 20 vision and the only glasses we wore was those cool sun glasses. And when we did need glasses, they had to be stylish. Of course we were paying for them ourselves and knew they gave us the look we wanted. It had to be classy, stylish and maybe sexy like one of the celebrities. If men wore those big framed glasses they were looked on as intelligent looking or sometimes sexy. Who knows? But for both sexes, as we got older, it was reading glasses. But you might be one that started out wearing glasses and gradually needed bifocals. One might say "I just need these for reading." And that was true for a while. Then later on, there were cataracts. The film growing over your eye making it difficult to see clearly. So you get them removed and you most likely can do without glasses. Have you ever noticed some older persons holding what they were reading so close to their eyes it may touch their nose? I have. It was many years ago when I was young and thought nothing about it until later in my years. Not for sure, but I don't think the eye doctors new all about the new discoveries way back then. Next came the contact lens. I've never worn them, so I can't give firsthand information. Unlike glasses, they don't hide the beauty of your eyes or slip down on your nose when you're in the middle of reading something important or trying to impress some one of the opposite sex. But, contacts do require a little daily care. Maybe after a while that is something you don't want to be bothered with. And find it easier to put on a pair of stylish glasses and keep going. Let me back up a little. You start off with needed glasses, then they had to be stylish, next contact lens and later maybe cataract removal. And it all comes down to what's important and what works for you. It's easy to see, the eyes have it.

Look at it this way

There was still room to meet someone new on my journey. This is true for all of us. The race doesn't matter, but rather what impression they may have made on you or you them. What is important is that our paths crossed. It may have been for only a short time, but time enough to add him, her or both to a limb or branch on my journey tree. Besides, I could learn something new and that's always a good thing. As you read some of all we talked about, you'll understand the heading;

"God is our Refuge and Strength."
I had a chance to meet and talk with a gracious couple who invited me into their home. I was given their names by one of my doctors and they agreed to talk with me. Even though they knew I was coming, the wife looked doubtful as she opened the door. We both laughed about it after a short while into my visit as I made myself comfortable on the couch. Both are in their eighties and have been married for forty years. After talking with me for a while, she left the room to see if her husband wanted to join us. He has had Parkinson for several years and was resting. When he came out, I explained to him what my book was about. The first thing he said was "Never say old because of the new life with God." He talked about his walk with God and how he stays connected to their church as much as possible. He is a college graduate and worked as an engineer and she was a medical technician. When his wife spoke up, she answered the

question about her journey and this is how she put it. "I guess I was forty when my journey started. There were so many things changing. Moving and traveling was one of them. We moved from New York to Florida to North Carolina and ended here in our own retirement home. Our first move that made an impact on my journey was leaving friends of forty years and a house we had lived in for nineteen. We have four children with careers and our daughter is married to a pastor. They are all within traveling distance some closer and some farther. She limits her driving only to places they need to be. She sounded confident when telling all she had to do for her husband and herself. She has help and visits at times from church members. She sometimes drove her husband to different appointments and found it difficult to manage getting him around. She manages to get them to church and members sometimes are there for help. The rest of my time spent with them talking about our children, some of our likes, our churches and other topics of interest.

Quick question and quicker response: After telling my male friend I was writing a book, I asked him this. How did you know you were on your journey to old age? Without hesitation, he answered, "When I wake up some mornings and think where did the time go?

Accepting change—One step at a time

As I continued to travel on my journey coming well into my sixties, I began to realize that some parts of my life were changing. After working for thirty years, work was no longer one of the main thoughts in my everyday living. Although, when it was, it was full of all that made me stronger and wiser. Therefore church was out most of the time. That being true, I realized there was so much more I could be doing. The first thought that came to my mind was traveling. Both of us made good on that promised. With so many changes starting to happen, I didn't want to think about getting old. I refused to let that word slow me down. New doors were opening that I never thought about. How about you, were you ready to accept the changes that getting older or being old would bring? Some changes were just a little harder to accept. The things you would normally do, now you need help. In my opinion, it's harder for some men. Why is it that the one item you need most in the grocery store is on the top shelf? The only way to get it is to ask for assistance from another customer. So, you need help. There are other things you can deny, like your weight, strength or even your height, but age may be a little hard to do. Sometimes we have to step back and listen to ourselves. Of course, it might not be what we want to hear. All that you can and cannot do comes to light. I am so happy and blessed that everything about being old is part of a special journey. Let's not concern ourselves with what we might not be able to do. Instead, go for all the things you can and want to do. The memories that may bring to mind those three stages again. Whether they are true for some and not for others, you choose to move on. Now might be a good time to look back at those three stages; resistance, denial and acceptance. You may or may not have experienced any of them. If so, think about them as being a part of your journey.

With growing comes adaptation

When someone is asked to tell about their journey to old age, it brings back memories from many years ago. Memories surfaces as far back as their youth to adult life to the present. Therefore this journey could have started at any stage and it becomes difficult to pinpoint where. As a person grows, their involvement in what is happening around them can and will make a big impact on their life. Somewhere in between, the realization of becoming older hits them. Now, wiser choices are made and the ability to get through difficult times increase.

This is some of how this friend tells about his journey. Perhaps leaving it up to us as readers to say or guess when he realized his journey was heading toward old age. I titled it: **"A Look Back at Years Gone By"**

> From infant until now, life's journey takes on many phases. Growing up in our neighborhood, our parents kept us pretty well "in tack" as we would say. Going to school from the first to the eight grade took on many aspects of my life. It was a period of adjustments; doing things you didn't necessarily like, meeting girls along the way. I mainly liked school studying and homework. Every day we had to walk to and from school. Around the 7th grade, we had to change

schools. The Lord was on our side as we moved from school to school. Shortly after graduating from High school and then working at an industry in town, I joined the military. It was the first time I had been away from home. My first experience with flying after joining the military was quite an adventure. Basic training came hard to some that enlisted, some wanting to go back home. I did miss home a little when the instructor talked about home. We were made to attend chapel service on Sunday. It was nothing like the worship service I was accustomed to. About 6 months before my enlistment time was up, I got married. I decided to let go of the military. After many years of marriage and with both our parents deceased, the church has become a solid rock we both can cling to. Up until now, this journey has been a rewarding one. There has been ups and there has been downs. God has been there for me three score and ten. He has been there in my up rearing. He has brought me through many toils. He was there when I went in places of danger. I recall seeing my mother on her knees, especially when things weren't going so well. She would start humming the old familiar hymns. The times when I first left home going into the military and going places I shouldn't have gone, God and my mother's prayers were there. We serve an awesome God, a forgiving God. And I made a vow to the Lord along the way that I would serve Him all the way till death.

Robert Carter/Morganton

Independence!

That's a difficult thing for me to even think about giving up. Driving comes to mind first, because already I am driving shorter distances and choose not to drive at night. But it's something about just being able to jump in your car and go where and when you like. Let me ask you this. Do you automatically get on the passenger side when you are going someplace with your child? Maybe I could learn how to sit back and relax, simply because I know that day is coming. I will sit on the passenger side and enjoy being driven around. Independence includes so much more, but let's talk about all the things we fill our days and some nights doing. We still have to cook, clean and all the other things if we want to continue living by ourselves. I don't think our children want to take our independence away, but rather wanting to take care of us. It's hard to make them understand. I had planned to get a medical alert system due to the fact that I climb stairs a few times a day to wash and just relax in the den while I'm downstairs then back up again to do something else. I waited too long and my children did it. ☺ Stand fast on your choices of what you are still able to do because who knows your body better than you and your doctor? ☺ I was thinking where to put this funny incident with my daughter but here seems the perfect place. I was visiting her church and we were on our way to another area of the church. She took hold of my hand and was leading me around behind her. I asked her how I was going to attract a man if she's leading me around like an old lady. I was, but the men didn't have to know it. After all I was looking good. We laughed about it together. When she tried it on another visit, I kept my hand out of her reach.

Remember When, While You Can

There was a time for a few years (2007 thru 2011) when some of my friends and I celebrated MLK Day. I hosted a luncheon complete with original games. The stipulation was you had to be 60 y/o or over. Each year I created a poem or reading for them as a way of welcoming them. This one was my favorite and I wanted to share it.

Remember When, While You Can
Created expressly for
Martin Luther King, Jr. Celebration Luncheon Friends 2011
By
Mary P's Thoughts Original

It's hard to believe how the time goes by, especially when you reach
our age
Our body changes, as well as our minds, but our memories fill page
after page
We wore homemade clothes and hand me downs, and knew that
we were cute
We wore miniskirts and a big ole afro with hair nappy right down
to the root

Underneath we wore what our mothers called bloomers, not a fancy
stich to be found

At times I thought Mama even made these, because the weight felt
close to a pound
Don't forget the houses we lived in and the wood stoves that kept
us from cold
No dryers then, we hung clothes on the line, these memories are
worth more than gold

Remember when, while you can
Your first time (I see you smiling), your first date and first real kiss,
these memories fade really slow
It's not the same as your first store bought dress, although both will
cause you to glow
Back when schools were for colored children only, to keep us apart
from the whites
Think of all the things that happened while we fought for our civil
rights
Some things at times will jog your memory; canning jars or picking
greens
Maybe even the wood sacks we carried to keep burning fire under
the beans
When I hear the song, "A Hole in the Wall," it brought to mind our
"hole in the ground"
I remember the outhouse was what it was named, but now our
choices are oval or round
Whatever else you can think of that happened way back then
My prayer for you is to *remember,* just as long as you can
This original reading composed just for you, so you can read it and
remember when
Add to it, laugh about it, talk about it, but do it while you still can

Ode to women over 65 or slightly over!

"Hoorah We Made It"

That's something to shout about, sing about and /or talk about to whomever will listen. It doesn't matter if it's funny or it might even be boring to some, but it's your story and there is not another one like it. Don't you think you could fill a book? To get to this stage in our life, can't you see yourself at times in a rocking chair humming your favorite song? What kind would it be? It could be an old love song that brings back memories of your first love or heart break, or that spiritual song that brings you close to tears of joy and thanks. For others it may have been when they held their first child in their arms. That was so long ago, but when you close your eyes it seems like yesterday. You wonder if you had it to do all over again, would you do it. Or better yet, would you have done it differently. I say, probably not. Everything that happened had a reason behind it and somewhere in the pages in this book it stood out or woke up that memory you had set aside. Whatever reasons that might be going through your mind, let them flow. Even with the struggles, disappointments and hardships, we can still rock in this chair and put a smile on our faces. When you think about it, you can remember the joy in-between that made it all worthwhile. And if someone ask why you are smiling to yourself, you simply tell them, "You had to be there." I come to the conclusion there is joy in aging and if you recall long and hard enough, you'll know what joy they're talking about.